UNLEASH YOUR CHILD'S POTENTIAL:

123 practical tips and useful strategies

Pam Goodman

Copyright © 2014 by Connectingthedots
Unleash Your Child's Potential:
What you can do
Pam Goodman
www.connectingthedotsforkids.com
pamgoodman11@gmail.com

Published 2014, by Light Messages
www.lightmessages.com
Durham, NC 27713
Printed in the United States of America
Paperback ISBN: 978-1-61153-113-8
Ebook ISBN: 978-1-61153-114-5

ALL RIGHTS RESERVED
No part of this publication may be reproduced, stored in a retrieval system, or transmitted in any form or by any means, electronic, mechanical, photocopying, recording, scanning, or otherwise, except as permitted under Section 107 or 108 of the 1976 International Copyright Act, without the prior written permission except in brief quotations embodied in critical articles and reviews.

www.connectingthedotsforkids.com

To my amazing children, I have been blessed to be your mom.

To the wonderful children, I have been honored to work with.

To those children needing a voice,
I hear you.

Acknowledgements

I would like to thank the children I have been so blessed to serve, as well as the many fine parents and professional educators with whom I have collaborated.

This book is comprised of 14 years of experience from moms, teachers, observation, trial and error, student input and validated research.

Special acknowledgement to Dr. Howard Gardner's *multiple intelligences* theory and valuable educational resources of *www.touchmath.com* and to *School House Rock.*

Contents

Acknowledgements	iv
Introduction	vii
Chapter 1 Target	1
Chapter 2 Visual	4
Chapter 3 Auditory	9
Chapter 4 Kinesthetic	12
Chapter 5 Verbal	14
Chapter 6 Musical	17
Chapter 7 Language	19
Chapter 8 Math	21
Chapter 9 Social	23
Chapter 10 Nature	24
Chapter 11 Whole Child	26
Chapter 12 Collaboration	28
Chapter 13 Real Life	34
Chapter 14 Environment	40
Chapter 15 Personalized	42
Chapter 16 Praise and Rewards	44
Chapter 17 Flexible	47
Chapter 18 Breaks	49
Chapter 19 Conclusion	52
About the Author	58

Introduction

Everyone has strengths and weaknesses, gifts and talents. Educating ourselves on how our children learn is a critical element to building confidence in our children's world. It is not just the teacher's job to understand. Parents are life educators and need to be valuable advocates. Three ways that you can immediately positively impact your child is:

1. **Collaborate**

   A skill needed for all adults involved to successfully teach both life and academic skills. Collaborating among partners, as well as collaborating with teachers. Your child learns every day by watching and experiencing each adult interaction. My hope is for all adults to collaborate openly with the ultimate goal of children:

   - comprehending how they learn
   - understanding what they need from their teachers
   - actively participating in their roles

   Any subject, task and life situation is achievable with the tools you have equipped your child with. What a gift to empower your child with the ability to deal with frustrations, persevere through any project and enjoy academic success.

2. **Empower**

   When children are taught how they learn, they feel empowered and self confident. Many experiences and research has been compiled to produce this book. Gathered in one place is learning styles, learning processes, learning structure and confidence building.

3. **Increase flexibility**

   Please be open to input and idea sharing. Because your child is a strong type of learner in one subject, it does not mean that they are the same type learner in all subjects. Nothing is bad or wrong, it just is. Using your child's strength in areas of weakness is a critical piece coupled with the attitudes of the adults involved.

   If your child senses there is something to be worried about because all the adults around them are worried about them, it feeds their anxiety.

   You will find this journey fascinating and will most likely uncover you and your partner's learning and processing styles. My combination is visual, auditory and social with verbal processing and structure. What's yours?

Chapter 1
Target

This book will enable parents and guardians to maximize the potential of their children. Teachers, students, and concerned citizens interested in finding a solution to today's educational situation will also benefit from the knowledge and experiences shared.

The goal is to facilitate collaboration; so, ultimately, the students reach their full potential. The skills learned can be applied to any learning endeavor of the child's daily life from life skills, academics to future employment.

To start, there is sometimes debate on who is the child's teacher. I would say both! The parents are the child's first teacher and the primary educator until the child enters preschool and kindergarten.

It is critical that the parents understand how their child learns. The child benefits with consistency and understanding; as well as having a valuable advocate for every grade level.

You will find many ideas and solutions in this book. The ideas are meant to inspire more ideas and provide limitless opportunities.

No matter who is the primary teacher, it is important for all parties to be on the same page.

Consider the following:

1. **Input**

    Both teachers must be open to collaborate and receive others' input. I know it is your child, but what the teacher sees is how the child exists in a larger peer centered environment without direct parental support.

2. **Feelings**

    Emotions may run high and feelings may get hurt. It is never the teacher's intention to hurt your feelings.
    Most teachers love their class and call them "their kids". I know he is your baby, but all teachers know that new skills require practice and without practice are never mastered.

3. **Your fears**

   Sometimes, unknowingly, you push your insecurities onto your child. Keep in mind, your child is always watching how adults handle situations. If you are worried about your child, they will feel that there is something to be worried about. If you feel like they should be entitled to preferential treatment, they will grow up feeling they should be entitled to special treatment. Funny as this may sound, but when it comes to their learning, it does not matter what you think or feel, but what they think and feel about it.

Through the collaboration of parents and teachers, this book will help empower young people to become independent, confident and successful learners. Ultimately, the children, understanding how they learn, will process and apply that knowledge to reach their full potential. This will prepare them to be strong contributors to society.

Chapter 2
Visual

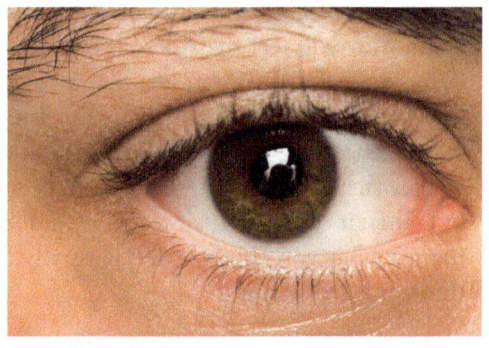

Many of us are visual learners. We need to see it to process it efficiently. Have you ever had someone tell you something, but you forget it a few minutes later? Have you ever had an image pop into your head over and over again? With technology today, we are almost forced to be visually focused due to all the creative and impulse driven strategies used to catch our attention.

Some common helpful tools for visual learners are:

1. **Visual only**

    Focus on the visual strength with a picture and utilize minimal talk and clutter.

2. **Simple**

    Simple instructions or rules used to memorize the steps in mastering concepts.

3. **Available resources**

    Tap into existing excellent educational videos, such as, *School House Rock* and *The Magic School Bus*.

4. **Organization**

    Organize information succintly. By taking lots of information and producing a graphic allows for visual learners to memorize facts without being overwhelmed with too much data. The visual "Gallon G" helps organize all the measurements needed for word problems and cooking recipes in a simple graphic visual. See how you can quickly recall that there are 4 quarts in a gallon and 2 pints in a quart. All of this information is located in one easy to remember visual.

5. **Computers**

    Utilize computer access with videos, YouTube, computer programs and Google images. Google Images is helpful for many subject areas, such as, vocabulary, math concepts, inferences, science and generating ideas for creative writing. Try it…type in a concept and check out the images.

Visuals are always at your finger tips IN your surrounding. Without having to make visuals or grab your computer, you can quickly and easily access your environment.

Some visual examples of ways you can access your environment to help master school concepts are:

6. **Perimeter and Area**

   For perimeter, point out baseboards around the room, edges of your table, border of your child's desk.

   The Area is the space covered with floor tiles or carpet, the surface of your table or your child's desk.

Many teachers use a football field for their sports fans. The outline is the perimeter. The playing field is the area.

7. **Inference**

   Use your coffee cup and have your child list what they are thinking when they see you sipping your coffee.

   Your child could infer that you are: sleepy, thirsty, enjoy the aroma, cold, fashionable, practical, busy... You can add to their list and generate even more ideas to nail down the concept of inferences.

   Modify it with what you are wearing, eating or buying.

8. Shapes

Circles can be easily found with a pizza pie, clock, wheels, buttons, smiley faces, door knobs, cupcakes and wheels.

Rectangles are sheets of paper, doors, bulletin boards, newspaper pages and lunch boxes.

Triangles are pizza and cake slices.

Next, once you are open to finding things in your environment, your child will start noticing things too. Make it a game and find things in the environment while driving in the car.

Chapter 3
Auditory

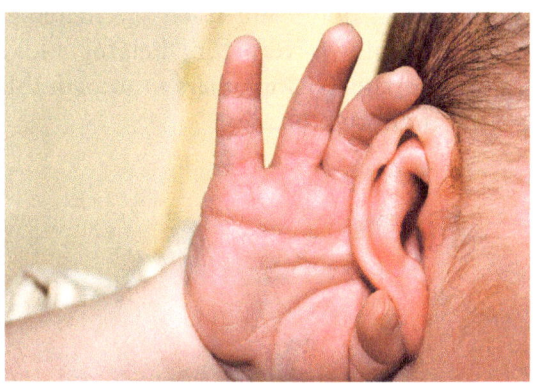

There are many auditory learners. We need to hear it to process it efficiently. Have you ever had someone tell you something and you can hear their voice pop into your head while you are working on a task?

Several excellent educational auditory strategies that facilitate this learning style include:

1. **Read along devices**

    Many libraries allow you to order read along series books on-line. They come on tape, CD and computer devices. Your child benefits by being able to continue their momentum with a favorite age appropriate series.

2. Engage the family

Kids like to be the teacher. While role playing, your child also hears the information. Allowing your child to be the teacher at home and teach the material to your family is very fun, helpful and age appropriate. Giving others a turn, continues the auditory process.

3. Read out loud

Embrace creativity and let your child read out loud to their favorite stuffed animal, pet or sibling. Reading should be fun.

4. **Songs**

    Videos, podcasts, YouTube and catchy tunes are entertaining and have an auditory focus, as well as visual. Allowing your child to personalize their own songs makes the activity high interest and encourages creativity.

5. **Focus**

    Have your child shut their eyes to remove distractions and focus on listening. While their eyes are shut, have them quietly repeat what you want them to process or memorize. Filtering distractions is an important life skill.

6. **Role play**

    Let your child practice facing the presenter or teacher; so, they learn how to focus on the important voice they need to hear.

7. **Empower**

    Encourage your child to repeat facts out loud. It is very important if they are also a verbal processor. When performing a task, "talking IN your head" is a learned skill. Whispering is another way to talk and get their needs met. Encourage positive self talk when locking in concepts.

CHAPTER 4
KINESTHETIC

Kinesthetic learners need to do it to process it efficiently. The child requires a hands-on, physical connection with the material.

Excellent educational tools for kinesthetic learners are:

1. **Manipulatives**

   They are hands on materials with moving parts. Being able to touch the work as you do it keeps your learner engaged and absorbing

2. **Physical body movement**

   Allow your child and your family to hold numbers in their hands. Let your child sort the numbers from highest to lowest while physically moving everyone to their proper spot. You can modify it with planets or any subject that requires organizing. Practice math facts while jumping on the trampoline or shooting hoops.

3. **Keyboarding**

   Using the computer and computer programs provide kinesthetic and high interest learning because they are touching the keyboard with their fingers while learning.

4. **Easy Access**

   High interest, colored manipulatives, like LEGO® are very helpful in solidfying math concepts.

5. **Clapping**

   Clapping out syllables are a fun way to facilitate spelling while maintaining alertness.

Chapter 5
Verbal

Verbal processors need to say it to process it efficiently. This is different than auditory learners because it is critical for your child to speak and not just hear.

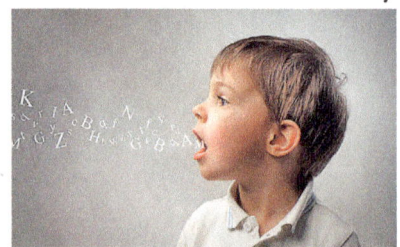

I have found a connection with visual and verbal processors where they both benefit greatly from looking at the flash card information while saying it.

Excellent educational strategies for verbal processors are:

1. **Social environments**

    There is a reason to speak. Verbal processors need to know that it is okay to speak out loud; even if, it is just a whisper. Once you know your child is a verbal processor, letting the teacher know is important because No Talking rules would be confusing for your child. Some students feel the need to verbalize, but do not want to disturb their classmates. It is important for them to know that many people are verbal processors and practicing whispering is a valuable skill. Again, a teacher will need to let the child know that it is okay to whisper in class. It is the teacher's classroom and the students know that they follow the teacher's rules at school. Most children will not let a teacher know this information. It may require a parent teacher conference.

2. **Practice**

    Encourage your child to repeat facts out loud. This skill is easy to apply to anything that could be written on a flash card, such as, math facts, vocabulary and test prep info.

3. **Double Checking**

    Verbal processors benefit from double checking that what they said is what they wrote down and not second guessing themselves. There are many verbal processing adults who do not know they are verbal processors. This information will enlighten many people.

4. **Role play**

    Provide situations where your child can talk it out. Let them be the teacher at home. They can make it fun by teaching a pet, favorite stuffed animal, sibling or parent. This method benefits auditory processors too.

5. **Math facts**

   Encourage using flashcards with the answer. When verbalizing the flash card, the entire math fact is absorbed. It almost becomes "one word" and makes recall easier. Initially, math facts are absorbed more efficiently, if the child looks at the math fact, such as, 6 + 2 = 8, and continues to look at it while speaking it 5 times.  They will know when it is absorbed because it becomes more natural to say. After 5 times, remove the visual and ask the fact. If the fact is not locked in, it requires an additional 5 times of looking at it while saying it. Afterwards, make practice even more fun, by adding bazillion to the end of a number, 6 bazillion + 2 bazillion = 8 bazillion

6. **Study buddies!**

   Social enhances verbal processing and is fun too. Bonus is the endorphins from having a friend over.

Chapter 6
Musical

Musical processors process information musically. Many children benefit from this method because it is age appropriate, catchy and uplifting.

Excellent educational strategies for musical processors include:

1. **Listening**

    Have your child experiment with listening to background music while learning or learning through instructional music.

    Since others may find the music distracting, using headphones and alternative methods will need to be considered.

Some musical learners can not filter background music. This requires some trial and error for each specific child. This is a time of observation. If your child is distracted or is abusing this privilege, you will need to take this option away.

2. **Educational songs**

    There are some great educational songs that are beneficial to many different types of learners. *School House Rock* targets many areas including musical, auditory, visual and high interest.

3. **Creativity**

    Children can make up their own songs. Have your child modify with their own lyrics. They can sing along to existing songs too. You will see what works for your child. When listening to their newly created song, you may uncover a step in a concept that is not locked in. Please do not correct your child if you uncover a problem, but log it in your mind to plan to teach at another time. You do not want to have your child associate a negative with a positive learning experience.

Chapter 7
Language

All of us have gifts and talents, strength and weaknesses. Using your gifts to master your weaknesses is a powerful skill.

If your child is gifted in language, using their language skills in all areas is critical, especially if they struggle in other areas.

Children gifted in language are able to utilize effectively:

1. **Acronyms**

    Encourage acronyms that are meaningful for them. Share the term, acronyms with a common one, such as, LOL (Laugh Out Loud). Apply one to their world, such as, G.B.D.F.A (Good Boys Deserve Fudge Always – for those learning music.).

Have your child make up their own acronyms to remember concepts. Being funny will help them remember; so, try not to stifle their creativity.

2. **Associations**

   Use associations, such as, "weird is weird because it is spelt weird." (It doesn't follow the i before e rule.)

3. **Real life**

   Math terms can be remembered through language versus pure memorization, such as:

   Pi is celebrated on
   March 14th at 1:59 pm
   (3rd month, 14th day at 1:59)
   = 3.14159

4. **Reading**

   Language learners find it easier to learn through reading.

Chapter 8
Math

Children gifted in math are logical. They appreciate and thrive in structure in both the school and home environment.

The following strategies help a child gifted in math:

1. **Schedule**

    A written schedule for homework that includes breaks allows your child to check off progress which is empowering for them. In the classroom and at home, a posted daily schedule with clear written instructions is calming and allows for the "newness" of the lesson to sink in without the distractions of needing to prepare for the unexpected.

2. **IF / THEN**

   Your child seeks reasoning and can apply techniques quicker when rules are applied.

3. **Money and Numbers**

   Because they are logical, there is an ease with numbers because they can find patterns and apply concepts. Formulas are con-crete. They are able to apply to real life since money is numerical and many life skills have some simple rules applied to them, such as, saving and spending.

4. **Planner**

   A person gifted in math is a planner by nature and one who prides himself on making sound decisions and following the rules.

   Even though, they would be able to learn from their mistakes, they will get frustrated when following the rules does not always provide their expected result. This is where you teach your child about realistic expectations and flexibility in life.

Chapter 9
Social

Dr. Howard Gardner has two categories for social. They are "people smart" and "self smart."

Those who are people smart like interaction which keeps the child engaged and provides the ability to learn from others. Even though they may learn from others, they are also able to accept and reject based upon their own experiences, opinion and reasoning skills. Group projects can be entertaining and motivating.

People who are intrapersonal learners are self motivated. They would prefer to learn on their own and are known to be thinkers. They will sometimes be frustrated with others because their prefcrence is to work alone.

Chapter 10
Nature

Children benefit from applying what they are learning to nature.

Dr. Howard Gardner has done research on naturalistic intelligence and found that children with naturalistic intelligence are fascinated with the seasons and weather.

Your child is sensitive to their surroundings. They are able to compare and contrast animal characteristics. Subjects can be tailored to nature because your child likes to explore nature.

Applying the lesson to the outdoors, could be done by applying letter recognition using fish types if your child loves fishing. Allow your child to seek out nature and collect sticks or rocks for math assignments.

Gardner found that children like to bring the outdoors in. For example, creating topographical maps make an indoor project feel like an outdoor project.

Careers for naturalistic intelligent individuals include astronauts, forest rangers, botanists and chefs.

Chapter 11
Whole Child

Because a child is gifted in one area or has a strong learning style, it does not mean that they do not need or benefit from multi-sensory techniques or use different learning styles with different subjects. Many students use visual and auditory tools, as well as process information verbally. Making learning high interest and age appropriate only helps solidify concepts for all types of learners and processors. There are many educational videos that teach to all levels because they are so high interest. *School House Rock* is a phenomenal educational tool because it reaches all types with its visuals, musical aspects, high interest and entertaining style. I am fascinated with how their songs touch almost every learning style and process from auditory to verbal processors if they sing along, with kinesthetic learners moving during the video and visual learners watching.

It is important for your child to be able to apply what they are learning to real life; so, it has meaning and recall feels natural. Once they uncover what works for them, they will share with you so much that it will make you smile every time. You should be proud of yourself and will develop a deep sense of pride on how valuable a role you played in your child's development.

Chapter 12
Collaboration

A key contributor to unleash your child's potential is the collaboration of the adults involved. The child benefits from everyone being on the same page. Both the grade level teacher and the parental teacher must be open to accept others' input and collaborate on a mutually agreed solution.

Some thoughts to consider when collaborating:

1. **Perception**

   A perception may be a reality in a different environment. Your child does not always behave the same at school as they do at home. It is a completely different environment. While most children are people pleasers, at school, there is a social and internal competition surrounded by a large number of peers and excessive structure, such as, the daily schedule. At home, there could be social and internal competition among siblings, but the environment is not as structured and your child is vying for your attention and not peer acceptance. Some kids talk up a storm at home, but hardly speak at school. When group instruction is necessary, rules must be made for times of No Talking. Sometimes it is difficult for children to make choices which might result in a consequence; so, they choose never to talk at school.

2. **Participation**

   Your child is an active participant but should never feel entitled. Entitlement does not prepare your child for adulthood. It is important for your child to build their own skills and learn how they learn surrounded by adults with positive and encouraging attitudes. Sometimes children do not know what their role is or why it is important. Filtering distractions is a learned skill. Teaching your child to focus on their work and ignore other distractions is difficult, but rewarding. If the teacher has prepared an excellent lesson, but your child is laughing at a classmate being silly and not paying attention, it is as if no lesson was prepared at all.

3. **Competing agendas**

   Open parents grow to become valuable advocates and strong supporters in their child's education. Your teacher has child development education and experience on her side. There is a lot you can learn from her.

   Most children are people pleasers and if the adults have competing agendas, the child is fed frustration and shame because they can not please all adults.

Competing life partner agendas also affect your child's self esteem just as much. Put your child's needs first.

Your child is very capable. Work on your own insecurities about your child without sharing them. Your attitude about your child's abilities has a profound impact on them.

Your job is to partner not unload unreasonable requests. The teacher's classroom has approximately 25 other students with a full agenda. She can not spend one-on-one time with your child all day.

4. **Mastering difficult concepts**

   When your child is having difficulty mastering a concept, partner with the teacher and the concept will be mastered. Guaranteed! It might take a little more time at home with real life application, but I have no doubt it will be mastered.

Double check your "can do" attitude before working on the concept. Collaboration could include teachers sending a visual sample of the lesson home. When the lesson is applied to your child's home life, the concept becomes more meaningful and easier to recall. This effort highlights to your child that the adults are on the same page.

5. **Motivators**

    What sparks your child? Motivators that work for your child should be shared with their teacher. If your child loves to be outdoors, a reward for completing a difficult task could be extra recess time. If a child enjoys social interactions, a reward could be lunch with a friend in the classroom. Communication and collaboration with every adult involved having an open mind only produces positive results for the child. Sometimes the child just requires more practice. That is not a problem, just a fact.

    When a teacher asks you to work on a skill at home, please do. Do not make it a problem or a negative for your child. Your child is the one who needs to know that you are proud of them and that learning new things is a part of life.

    If you have a problem dealing with frustration, your child might to. Maybe it will be a new skill that you both learn together?

6. **Role modelling**

   Remember, your child is always watching and learning from the adults in their life. How you collaborate with your partner, teacher, boss and friends is noticed. Learning from others is a skill you would be teaching when you collaborate with your partner on how they learned a concept. Your partner might have learned the concept a different way. Neither way is right or wrong.

7. **Choice**

   Choice is a powerful tool to foster your child's potential. Empowering your child to make healthy decisions supports their buy in and builds their confidence.

   Include choice in homework where your child understands their responsibility and has some control on when, how and where they do their homework. To ensure you are respected and do not feed your own resentment, do not include choices that do not work for you or your family's schedule.

   Any time, you can praise your child for making good decisions that builds them up. Many children know their parents love them, but do not always know their parents are proud of them.

Feeling the natural consequences of decisions and learning from and not feeling shame for them is so developmentally healthy.

8. **Homework**

    If homework causes a lot of hassles for your family, please research my *Homework Hassles* book with simple tips and strategies to take the hassles out of homework.

9. **Practice**

    Collaboration is a skill that your child will use throughout their life in any situation. Practicing it as a child, only improves their flexibility and communication skills. What a skill to bring to any relationship, job or future endeavor. Your child is a child. This skill might be difficult and would benefit from an age appropriate reward system.

Chapter 13
Real Life

Some students have the ability to generalize concepts in all their environments. This is an important skill and one to be taught if it does not come naturally. Concepts become meaningful when they are meaningful in your child's world.

All school subjects can be applied to real life situations. When a concept is not mastered, practicing it in their environment creates understanding and builds confidence. It is important not to add more events to your life and apply concepts to activities you are already doing. Adding stress to any situation is not beneficial.

Here are some simple ways you can add concepts to your daily life:

1. **Grocery store**

    How many times do we go to the grocery store? This environment is chock full of opportunities to practice many concepts.

    - counting how many items are placed in the cart
    - weighing produce
    - finding sight words
    - identifying letters

Unleash Your Child's Potential

- reading labels
- observing the shopping cart wheels in motion
- estimating how much something will cost
- finding shapes
- writing out the grocery list

2. Elapsed time

Elapsed time can be practiced anytime, anywhere.

A. Car ride

How many times do we have to go somewhere like a birthday party, grocery store, park, pool or child centered activity? Every time you get in the car. Mark the time you get in the car to the time when you arrive. Calculate how long it took. You child will soon understand elapsed time.

B. In the house

Make it fun by setting the timer when your child starts brushing their teeth to when they are finished. Let them time you! They'll come up with the ideas soon. Don't be surprised if they time how long it takes you to tie your shoes or make them a sandwich.

C. Outside

Have a race in the yard. Time them when they get the mail, ride their bike or play basketball.

D. High interest

Measure how long it took to watch their favorite TV program or play their video game.

3. Practice

While riding in the car, your child can utilize time to get some practice in.

- Review flash cards.
- Handwrite with portable dry erase boards left in the car.

- Point out shapes in nature.
- Search for vocabulary words and letters on street signs and numbers on speed limit signs.
- Listen to educational songs.

4. **Measurements**

They can practice measuring by recording how tall each family member is in feet and inches and then in centimeters and meters. Let them be silly and measure their dog, a banana, toothbrush and their shoes.

5. **Cooking**

Involve your children with meal preparation. Concepts can be mastered, such as, cups, gallons, pints, quarts, colors, shapes and counting out items. Reading is enhanced when following directions. Remember, pick activities that you are already doing and do not produce stress. If you don't have time for them to do an activity, do not offer it as a choice. You do not want to associate a negative educational experience with an optional activity.

6. **Food**

Meal time can easily be a place where fractions can be found.

   A. **Pizza**

   One slice of pizza is usually 1/8 of the pie. They can see that eight slices equals one whole pie. That will visually lock in the concept for them that 8/8 = 1.

   B. **Shapes**

   Notice the shapes. At lunch, how many circles do you have on your plate. Don't forget to include your peas and grapes!

   C. **Math**

   Count your peas. Divide them into 2 equal groups.

7. **Games**

   Playing games with the family is a fun way to learn. Excellent educational games to play include Pay Day, Monopoly, Yahtzee, Scrabble, and Chess. Yahtzee solidifies math facts while teaching social skills.

   Excellent activities to play outside include: hop scotch, basketball, counting rocks and people.

8. **Flexibility**

   Any school concepts can be applied to their life. Just open your mind to the possibility. Soon, your child will be finding ways to share their knowledge. Involving your child and making it age appropriate, fun and even funny are simple ways to lock in concepts. To keep everyone's stress levels down, do not add more projects to your to do list.

9. **Relax**

   Don't forget to let it go sometimes. Everyone needs a break and we all need to relax and enjoy life too. Sometimes, we just need processing time and to "sleep on it". It will come. If your child sees you worried about them, they will think there is something to be worried about. Don't feed their anxiety with your anxiety.

Chapter 14
Environment

A calm environment is a critical element to learning. If something is difficult, having tasks organized and in a calm environment, allows all energy to be focused on the difficult task without distractions.

Here are some tips to use to add structure to your home:

1. **Written schedule**

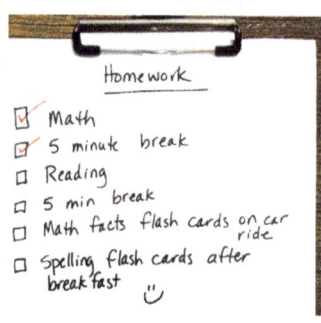

Many people benefit from a written schedule. It is very important for the school day, but is extremely helpful with homework and projects. Empowering your child by letting them check off items from the list highlights progress and provides positive self motivation. Don't forget to include breaks. Having an open mind to a schedule where items, like flash cards, are moved to the morning after breakfast when the mind is fresh, gives everyone a break and is more productive.

2. **Color**

    There is a lot of power in color. Using different colors helps to separate key areas. Colors can be used to highlight areas needing more effort.

    Blue is a memory color.

    Red is the secondary memory color.

    Always consider using **your child's favorite color** to empower them and keep them focused. I find using black for the basics and **color** for the steps provides instant clarity.

    If your child is having difficulty with spelling, use blue for the letters they are having difficulty remembering.

    Do the same for math to highlight a step in blue to help your child notice and absorb the step.

No clutter, calm environment, organized and colorful are keys to learning something new and difficult.

Chapter 15
Personalized

A quick and easy way to add interest to any subject is to use you child's favorite colors and topics. It is easier to remember something when it is of great interest to you.

Consider these high interest, age appropriate strategies that you can use:

1. **Favorite character**

    Applying what they are learning to their favorite character. Thomas the Tank Engine, Dora the Explorer, Super Mario and Super Heros puts concepts into their world and keeps them engaged.

2. **High interest items**

    Using age appropriate items and non-traditional items makes learning extra fun. Try using your child's favorite treat, such as, m&ms to understand a math concept where they could be rewarded with eating them.

3. **Age appropriate creativity**

   It is fun for children to role model. Let your child take on the job as the teacher and teach you, their siblings, their pets and their favorite stuffed animals. Ensure they know that it is a privilege and take it away if it becomes a distraction or an avoidance tactic.

4. **Favorite toy**

   Allow your child to choose their favorite toy to master concepts. Many people use LEGO® to learn math.

5. **Shopping**

   Have your child estimate how much they can buy for $10 without using a calculator. Give an example of $3.99 being almost $4 which covers two items with money left over is needed for tax. They will quickly see the benefit of estimating.

6. **Role playing**

   You can role play any situation in your home. Your child loves your attention. Pretend to go shopping. You will notice that the higher the interest level for your child, the more relevant and easier it is for them to process the information.

Chapter 16
Praise and Rewards

Praise for a specific skill, such as, reading directions out loud. Check with the teacher to ensure you are on the same page for skill mastery. If your teacher ever asks you to work on a skill with your child, please do it. It will benefit your child.

Some thoughts to consider about praise and rewards:

1. **Proud**

    Most children know their parents love them. Not all children know that their parents are proud of them. Please tell them and leave them notes. Trust me. They will love it!

2. **Mistakes**

    Praise for practice and not for perfection. We are a performance driven society. The end of grade tests feeds performance anxiety. As parents, we need to praise for effort, practice and not perfection. Perfectionism feeds insecurity and strengthens performance anxiety. Everyone has strengths and weaknesses. Your child needs to understand that.

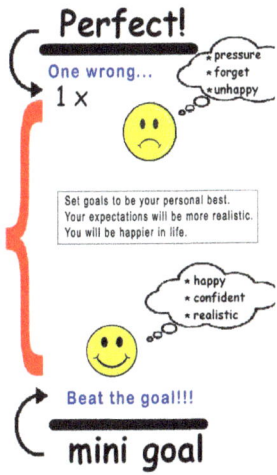

3. **Goals**

Your child benefits from learning how to deal with frustrations and setting goals that they can achieve. It does not mean if they are slow at a concept now that they will be slow at the exact same concept later.

4. **Anxiety**

Ensure that you are not feeding any anxiety by making their frustration your frustration. Positive, encouraging and calm are some key elements to model. Never limit your child by pushing your insecurities onto your child. There is nothing your child can not do. Nothing! You just need to set achievable goals and break it down if they need to learn it in smaller chunks.

5. **Attention**

   One of the best rewards you can give your child is your undivided attention. If able, spend one-on-one time with your child. Experts recommend 20 minutes a day. Turn your phone off. It needs to be undivided attention. Spending 20 minutes responding to texts is detrimental and sends the message to your child that your texts are more important than time with them. Free time to do something they love to do is another easy reward that is positive and motivational.

6. **Celebrate!**

   Celebrate how proud you are of your child. Many of us do not stop to celebrate our own accomplishments. Enjoying the rewards of your efforts is confidence building and encourages goal setting.

Chapter 17
Flexible

It is much easier to change your child's attitude if you are able to change your own attitude. We all make choices every day. You are a role model for your child and if you are easily frustrated, modeling how to calm down is a critical life skill. Your child is always watching and learning from adults in every situation.

Ways to add flexibility to your day:

1. **Car rides and white boards**

    Who says learning is supposed to be boring and unpleasant? Allow your child to activate their creativity. White boards are fun ways to add color and creativity to any assignment. After a day of pen and paper, let your child use whiteboards. They are smooth surfaced, portable and easy on the hands. They are flexible in that you can keep them in the car and bring them out whenever there is time waiting in the car and the child would like to practice writing, drawing or math facts. They also include the fun elements of color and choice.

2. **Focus**

   Studies have been done on the effects of chewing gum and peppermint on the mind and its ability to enhance concentration and focus. If your child abuses the privilege, take it away. If you notice it helps, keep it on hand.

3. **Endorphins**

   Stop for a minute and just enjoy your child. Kids are funny. Laughing is endorphin making. Why not teach the love of learning? The next chapter will talk about breaks and effective ways to include them that include generating endorphins.

Chapter 18
Breaks

Breaks are an important part of life. Just because you are not focusing on a task, does not mean your mind is not processing information. Some people think clearer about a problem after a good night's sleep. When working on homework or school projects, ensure everyone gets some endorphins.

Some quick break ideas are:

1. **Laughing**

    Do a couple knock knock jokes or share a funny story. Some kids require structure.

You might state that you get to tell 2 knock knock jokes before they tell 2 jokes.

2. **Exercise**

   Let them run around the house. Take 10 shots at the basketball hoop. Skateboard for 5 minutes.  Whatever it is, agree to it upfront.

3. **Muscle tightening**

   Show your child how to tightly make a fist, hold for a few seconds and then fully release their grip. Hold and release 5 times. This is a skill that they can take to school and do at their desk if they ever need some quick endorphins. Mention to your teacher that you taught them this skill. She might wonder? They have this skill available to them at any time and can always compress and release their grip in their pockets or in their desk if they feel self conscious. Try it! The body is a fascinating thing.

4. **Foods**

   Sometimes your child loses focus because they are hungry or thirsty. Certain foods are known to provide alertness, such as, peppermint and chewing gum. Let them have a snack and get a drink of water.

5. AM versus PM

Different times of the day are better than others. Doing flash cards in the morning when their mind is fresh is helpful. When there is free time in a car ride, fit in practice without having to schedule more things into your day.

6. Choice

If time permits, let your child choose when a break can occur, such as, before or after a favorite activity. Agree upon the amount of time, then have your child, set the timer. If your child abuses the privilege, take the privilege away from them.

Chapter 19
Conclusion

You are your child's most important and valuable advocate. If you do not believe in your child, how can you expect someone else to?

Key points to remember:

1. **Your child's participation**

    Every child is capable of learning. Your child needs to be educated on their part. If your child is taught how they learn and they do their part to process the information, you will see them blossom. If they are a verbal processor and they do not verbalize the information, then that is only in their control. If they are a visual learner and they do not look at the lesson, then they do not absorb the lesson.

2. **Your valuable advocacy and support**

    If you understand how your child learns, you are a valuable contributor to your child's education. Your communication with the teacher and your support in their learning at home will do nothing but build your child's confidence.

3. **Your child's teacher**

   Once a teacher knows how a child learns, she will commit to it. A teacher loves her class and calls them, "her kids". You won't find a more invested adult in your child's progress.

4. **Your understanding**

   Teachers have a multitude of students with a very full agenda. They can not spend one-on-one time with every child in the class for long periods of time. If they knew what you knew and you both partnered together, you will see a different child.

5. **Communication**

   Teachers can not read your mind or your child's mind. Healthy communication provides information not criticism. If your child is a visual learner, but the homework did not provide a visual sample, the teacher needs to know your child struggled. A teacher would never intentionally set up to dillute your child's learning. Re-teaching sheets can be sent home. Upfront agreed upon parent sign-off can be discussed when effort has been made, but homework is still too challenging. There are many options and resources available to the teacher, but if you do not communicate, she will not know.

6. **Anxiety**

   Most children are people pleasers and having competing agendas with adults involved in their lives can only produce stress. Stress does not foster learning. When a person is stressed, they lose their train of thoughts and ability to process information effectively. Work hard for all adults to stay focused on the same page.

7. **Love of learning**

   If your child desires to please you or your teacher too much, they will place an unhealthy pressure on himself to perform. That choice creates anxiety which affects learning. You need to monitor that you have a lighter attitude with your child. Note that some things just require more practice and that it is not a problem, just a fact.

8. Goals

We all want your child to progress. The person who wants it the most is your child. Small achievable goals build confidence. Perfectionism feeds low self esteem because they will never be satisfied. Please praise them for effort and progress not perfection.

9. Mutual respect

Always consider everyone's responsibilities and feelings about your child's success. Everyone is invested and has strong feelings about their performance; especially your child. Their job is a student. Who wants to feel like they are failing at their job every day?

Role	**Responsibility**
Teacher	Grade level
Parent	Life contributor/ Valuable advocate
Student	Active participant

Your child is watching. Teach them how to solve a problem with collaboration and team building. You are ALL on the same side.

I am very proud of your desire to be the best parent you can be. Once you apply the strategies in this book, you will relish in a profound sense of pride and joy. I smile in anticipation.

For more information, downloadable content, apps, workshops, blog, consulting, checklists, tutoring, educational tips and strategies, preschool through high school resources, go to:

www.connectingthedotsforkids.com

About the Author

For as long as she can remember, Pam Goodman has been fascinated with the process of learning. Born in Ontario, Canada, Pam graduated with degrees in business and education from the University of Albany and an MBA from Meredith College. Her rewarding work with families, teachers, and schools has inspired her to create Connecting The Dots for Kids (connectingthedotsforkids.com) as well as share her knowledge through books, educational consulting, and workshops. Pam is the proud mother of two amazing children, enjoys traveling, and currently resides with her family in Durham, NC.

CPSIA information can be obtained at www.ICGtesting.com
Printed in the USA
LVOW02s2052230714
395653LV00007B/119/P